Pop! Pop! Pop!

Ring! Ring!

Mum is going to cook
some popcorn.

She gets a big pot and tips a
bit of oil into the bottom of it.

3

Dad sees the packet
of popping corn. He
looks into the pot.

"It needs corn," he
thinks. He tips some in.

Sam comes in and peeks
into the pot. He thinks,
"That's not much corn."

So he adds a lot of
corn to the pot.

Mum picks up the packet.
She drops the rest of the
popping corn into the pot.

Then she sticks the lid on
and gets the pot hot.

Then there is a "Pop!"

And then "Pop! Pop!"

The popcorn keeps
popping and expanding.

Then "Pop! Pop! Pop! Pop! Pop! Pop!"

The lid of the pot lifts
up and Mum grabs it.

Popcorn spills out of
the pot and some
shoots up into the air!

Mum is in shock and yells to Dad, "Quick! Help me with all this popcorn!"

Dad tips popcorn into a dish.
Then he fills up a bigger dish.

Mum says, "This is one BIG popcorn snack! Munch on! We have lots to go!"

Words to blend

cook	looks	shoots
popcorn	corn	oil
sees	needs	peeks
keeps	grabbed	slammed
problem	bring	crack
help	step	thrill
drops	stick	end

Before reading

Synopsis: Mum is cooking popcorn but the family think that there isn't enough in the pot. What will happen when the corn begins to pop?

Review graphemes/phonemes: oo oo or oi ee air

Story discussion: Look at the cover and read the title together. Ask: *What is happening in the cover picture? What do you think will happen in this story?* Discuss children's experiences of helping make (or eating) popcorn, and share their predictions for what might happen.

Link to prior learning: Display a word with adjacent consonants from the story, e.g. *snack*. Ask children to put a dot under each single-letter grapheme (*s, n, a*) and a line under the digraph (*ck*). Model, if necessary, how to sound out and blend the adjacent consonants together to read the word. Repeat with another word from the story, e.g. *sticks*, and encourage children to sound out and blend the word independently.

Vocabulary check: expanding – getting bigger

Decoding practice: Display the word *expanding*. Show children how to split it into syllables (*ex/pand/ing*) and then sound out and blend each syllable in turn in order to read the word.

Tricky word practice: Display the words *some* and *comes*. Read the words and ask children to show you the tricky bit (*o-e*, which makes the sound /u/). Practise reading and spelling the words.

After reading

Apply learning: Ask: *Did you predict that the family would end up with too much popcorn? Or did you think things might go wrong in another way? Did the ending surprise you?*

Comprehension

- Who started making the popcorn?

- Who else added popcorn to the pot?

- Do you think it was a problem that they ended up with a LOT of popcorn? Or was it a good thing? What makes you think that?

Fluency

- Pick a page that most of the group read quite easily. Ask them to reread it with pace and expression. Model how to do this if necessary.

- Encourage children to read Mum's words on page 14, with lots of appropriate expression and urgency.

- Practise reading the words on page 17.

Tricky words review

going	comes	she
oh	into	out
he	all	have
go	says	we
some	there	so